Acknowledgments

It is a testament to Jack himself that everybody I approached for help with compiling this book agreed without hesitation.
Owners, trainers, grooms, vets and photographers all contributed to the story.

The stunning pictures, which to me are the heart of the book, have been provided by Fiona Scott-Maxwell, Ian Lamprell,
Kit Houghton, Tony Meredith, Joanna Prestwich, Horse & Hound/Trevor Meeks, Catherine Cawdron, Stewart Golder, Fiona Saxby
and David Edney. Without them there would have been no book.

Huge thanks go to Louise Lewis, whose knowledge of the publishing industry prevented me from tripping up on my first foray into both book
authorship and book publishing. She has also, along with Jennifer Hewitson and Kathryn White, read through countless drafts and final proofs.

Heartfelt thanks also to Nicki Averill, our designer, for her skill and enormous enthusiasm.

Finally, special thanks to Jeanette for entrusting this book to me. I feel enormously privileged to have been given the opportunity
to write about the irreplaceable and remarkable Jack.

Hilary Manners

———⇒•◦•⇐———

Copyright © Hilary Manners 2008

First published in 2008 by
Eventing Worldwide
Corner House, Normanton-on-Cliffe, Grantham, Lincolnshire NG32 3BH
Tel: 01400 250472
www.eventingworldwide.com

A CIP catalogue record for this book is available from the British Library

ISBN 978-0-9559524-0-1

Designed and typeset by Nicki Averill Design and Illustration
Cover photo by Fiona Scott-Maxwell
Printed in Belgium by Proost

OVER TO YOU

**Written by Hilary Manners
with Jeanette Brakewell**

Enjoy it!
Jeanette &
Jack.

eventing
worldwide
www.eventingworldwide.com

Contents

Saddle Up for Spinal Research

We horse riders are just so passionate about our sport, aren't we? There's such a strong bond between horse and rider. Riding is enjoyed both at the very highest level of competition and with a peaceful hack in the countryside.

Riders love what they do, but unfortunately 800 people a year are paralysed in the UK and too many of these are from riding accidents. Paralysis does not only mean not being able to walk again, but can also mean loss of movement in arms and hands, the inability to breathe on your own and perhaps the worst, the loss of independence.

The charity Spinal Research is giving hope to people who are paralysed. Established in 1980, we have developed into one of the leading international charitable organisations funding vital research into spinal cord repair.

In 2000 we launched our Saddle Up campaign specifically for the equestrian community, and with its help we have so far raised over £750,000 for vital research to get people walking again and back on their horses.

Our research never stops. In order to pay for it we rely totally on our supporters. Events are a great way to raise funds – a clear round competition, a sponsored ride, a lecture demonstration or simply a coffee morning. All of these and more are wonderful ways to support the Saddle Up campaign. They're great fun too!

We are very proud to be supported by Jeanette, who is a wonderful spokesperson for the Saddle Up campaign and is helping us to promote our crucial research. We are also supported by our Patron Ginny Elliot MBE and our Ambassador Francis Whittington, but you too can also play your part.

To help us beat paralysis and remove this threat from a sport that you love call 01483 898786, email saddle-up@spinal-research.org or visit our website www.spinal-research.org.

Isabel Robinson

Isabel Robinson
Specialist Fundraiser

Charity number 281325

6

Foreword by Yogi Breisner

Over To You. No horse deserves to have a book written about him more than he does. Together with Jeanette Brakewell they formed a very special partnership, a rare partnership that you only very occasionally get in equestrian sport when a horse and human work together as one.

If talent, flair, ability and consistency are the ingredients needed to be a top athlete then Over To You has them all. His international team record was outstanding and will be very hard for any equine athlete to equal, never mind beat.

As a pathfinder for the British Event Team on so many occasions the responsibility was on his and Jeanette's shoulders to give the whole team a good start. This is why he is so suitably named. It often was 'over to him' to come up with the goods, and he invariably did so.

One of my fondest memories of Over To You was at the Sydney Olympics, my first Championship as Team Manager. I can still picture him appearing over the brow of the hill to complete his cross country round, clear inside the time. No Team Manager could have had a better start. Little did I realise then that he was going to be such a vital part of the team for the next number of years.

It is proof of his strength and constitution, and Jeanette's excellent training and preparation of him, that he has stayed sound, fit and healthy for so many years as a top international event horse. His consistent performances gave everyone a bench mark to aim for. He was reliable in all three phases, but I think the cross country was where he really came to the fore. Being a thoroughbred he just loves to gallop and jump. His cross country round at the 2001 European Championships in Pau was pure poetry in motion, and I still use the video of it as an educational tool when discussing what cross country is all about.

I am sure you will enjoy reading about this unique animal's life, and travelling the same journey that he has done. Everyone whose life he has touched will always remember him due to his unassuming and tremendously big character. It has been an honour and a pleasure to have been associated with Over To You, and this book will ensure that his memory will live forever.

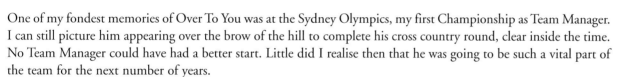

The early years

Over To You (Jack) was bred in the Spring of 1988 by Mary Lett in County Wexford, Ireland, out of her mare Another Miller. She remembers him well. "He was the most straightforward foal. With his sire Over The River's reputation that surprised me, but he was a little angel. We would always catch the foals when they were a day or two old, lead them around a bit, pick up their feet and get them used to being rubbed all over – though they probably didn't see a brush unless they were off to the sales! Jack was easy to teach and I was surprised when I heard he had been tricky to back – maybe that was the Over The River genes coming through. He had the end stable here I remember… it's hard to believe what he went on to do."

Within six months Jack was gone, sold with another thoroughbred foal by Mandalus after Michael Hickey, who stood Over The River, brought legendary racehorse dealer Tom Costello to see them – Tom tended to buy all the Over The River progeny. "I then never heard another thing! I'd checked race entries when Jack was at the right age to see if he was running but there was nothing. When I saw Tom one day much later I asked him what had happened to my Over The River foal. 'Oh, he was no good', came the answer.

"A few years later Lucy Hickey called me out of the blue: 'Did you know that the Over The River horse you bred

"He was the most straightforward foal. With his sire Over The River's reputation that surprised me, but he was a little angel."

Mary Lett on her farm in County Wexford, Ireland with some of her 2008 youngsters

Jack as a two year old, at home with the Cleggs

10

is currently at the Sydney Olympics?' Well, we were delighted, it was such a thrill – we had feared he might have ended up in a can or something!"

Mary still breeds from the beautiful farm she moved to on her marriage to Jack Lett in 1965. Horses are a way of life for her – despite being the top side of 70 years old she had 22 horses in her care last winter, and to discover Jack's success has been a huge source of pleasure and pride to her. Having not seen Jack since she sold him at six months old Mary was reunited with him at Tattersalls Horse Trials in his final season.

Tom Costello sold Jack on, as a two year old, to Tony Clegg. With excellent breeding for a steeplechaser he was one of three potential racers to enter Clegg ownership together. Tony's daughter Fiona recalls that despite their best efforts with plenty of good food he always remained, "a weedy youngster. Jack was very playful in the field; I remember one snowy day sledging down the field at Bramham, where we lived at the time, with him in hot pursuit trying to get his front feet onto the back of the sledge! Even as a two year old you could see his athleticism. He could, and often did, jump off all four feet like a cat."

In 1991 the Cleggs moved to Whixley Hall and Jack was sent to Tom Tate's racing yard. "He didn't seem to be particularly scopey and was a bit on the small side to race," Tom says, "but Over The River progeny are top class jumpers." He failed to impress amongst the batch of youngsters then in training, and that same year was sent to the Doncaster Sales, but returned to Whixley Hall rather in disgrace, having failed the vet.

It was Irish event rider Jonty Evans who took on the task of backing Jack effectively, racing methods not having proved particularly successful. Jonty was working for Tony Clegg at the time and one morning saw a new horse out in the field. "What's that?" he asked. "That's Mad Jack," came the reply, "no-one can break him properly… play around with him if you like."

Jack's first stable on Mary Lett's Wexford farm

"Even as a two year old you could see his athleticism.

He could, and often did, jump off all four feet like a cat."

11

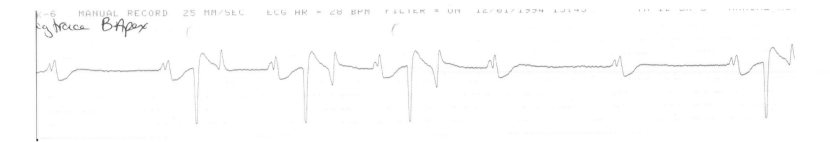

K-6   MANUAL RECORD   25 MM/SEC   ECG HR = 28 BPM   FILTER = ON   12/01/1994 13:43

g trace BApex

Pictured above a Base-apex ECG recorded at rest on 12.01.94

Jack suffers from a second degree atrioventricular block. The ECG shows two blocked beats for every three conducted beats

In 1992 Jack was occasionally heard to block three beats

Jonty, who has always favoured the 'traditional methods' of backing, started handling the then four year old, long reining him round the lanes and lungeing him. He found Jack not mad at all: Jack had picked up the nick name Mad Jack on his return to the Cleggs in light of stories of some shenanigans with stable lads, now forgotten. Instead he was so straightforward that the first time Jonty sat on his back there was no-one else around. "I simply climbed onto a tractor tyre and got on. Jack was good as gold. It was just old-fashioned breaking – no one had done that for him before. I think that if you do things properly you are rarely going to have a problem with a young horse. My main memory of him from those days was his real strong sense of curiosity and love of life. It's in his nature to always want to look around the next corner."

According to Fiona it was Jonty who impressed upon her father the depth of Jack's ability, and the horse was viewed by a couple of top event riders in Yorkshire with the hope that one of them would take him on. Both rejected him out of hand as not having good enough paces.

Fiona and Jonty then took Jack up to The Royal (Dick) School of Veterinary Studies in Edinburgh to have his unusual heart condition investigated (the reason for his having failed the vet at the Doncaster Sales). With a referral from the Clegg's vet Anthony Stirk, Jack was seen by both Karen Blissitt and Lesley Young. Karen explains: "Back in 1992, when I first saw him, we knew much less than we know now. Horses routinely miss maybe one heart beat in every four or five; it's their way of controlling their blood pressure. Jack normally missed two, followed by three beats, followed by two missed beats; occasionally he was missing three out of every six. This was unusual. His resting heart rate was very low, around 18 because of the number of missed beats. A 'normal' fit horse would have a resting heart rate of around 28 to 40."

However it was not just an unusual heart beat that Jack could boast: he also had a heart murmur caused by a leak in the main left sided valve of the heart. At that time it was not known that such heart murmurs could develop in response to training, and that they could sometimes go away when the horse was retired. Abnormalities of the left heart valve were then always thought to deteriorate over time and they are still one of the commonest causes of heart failure in horses.

Karen revealed that, "Sixteen years after we first saw him Lesley has recently published a paper into the effect of heart murmurs on performance, concluding that often there is no effect. However, we did not know that at the time." Jack's case was unusual enough to send his results to Professor John Bonagura of Ohio State University, one of the leading experts in the field.

Jack returned to the Royal (Dick) Veterinary Centre at Easter Bush two years later and produced very similar readings. "We decided that, although unusual, these were probably 'normal' results for this horse, as was the fact that his ECG readings were slightly bigger than standard. By then the horse was competing and there had been no deterioration in his condition," Karen Blissitt concludes.

THE PROPERTY OF MR T. CLEGG

102
Non VAT

CHESNUT GELDING
1988

{ Over the River (Fr.) { Luthier { Klairon
{ { { Flute Enchantee
{ { Medenine { Prudent
{ { { Ma Congaie
{ { Gala Performance { Native Dancer
{ Another Miller { { Red Letter Day
{ (1980) { Chillaway { Arctic Slave
{ { { Freezaway

This gelding has been broken and ridden away. Likely high-class N.H. prospect. Only being sold as the owner is leaving racing. Sold with a Pre-Sales Veterinary Certificate.

1st Dam
ANOTHER MILLER ran a few times at four years in Ireland.
Dam of:
    1986 f. by Gleason.
    1988 c. by Over the River (Fr.) (see above).

2nd Dam
CHILLAWAY, placed second over hurdles at three years.
Dam of **one winner**:
    Danny Harrold, two I.N.H. flat races at five years, 1989, also winner over hurdles in 1990 and placed to 1991, including second in Waterford Crystal Supreme Novices Hurdle, Cheltenham, **L**, and Kingwell Hurdle, **L**, in 1991, also won two point-to-points in 1989.
    Noelbonne Femme; broodmare.
        Roamaway; dam of
        Mandy Miller, an I.N.H. flat race in 1991.

3rd Dam
FREEZEAWAY ran a few times.
Dam of **four winners**:
    GOLDEN FREEZE, an I.N.H. flat race at five years, 1984, and placed, also won five races over hurdles, 1987–88, and placed four times including fourth in Sean Graham Brown Lad Handicap Hurdle, and won six races over fences, 1988–89, including Irish Life Assurance Nas Na Ri Chase, **L**, Sandeman Handicap Chase, Liverpool, Warwick Premier Chase, Warwick, placed five times including second in Mackeson Gold Cup Handicap Chase, **L**, third in Arlington Premier Series Chase Final, Cheltenham.
    Tom Miller, on the flat in 1982 and placed in 1984, also won three races over hurdles in 1982 and placed five times to 1983, also winner of three races over fences, 1983–84, and placed 10 times to 1985 including second in Guinness Handicap Chase, Punchestown, **L**, Northern Telecom Handicap Chase, Galway, **L**, and Navan Supporters Troytown Handicap Chase, Navan, **L**, also won a point-to-point in 1982, also four races over fences in USA, including in 1991.
    Baybush, winner and placed over hurdles at five years, 1986.
    The Chiller, two races over hurdles and placed, also placed on the flat.
    Chillaway (see above).
    Waltzaway, placed second over hurdles at five years, 1985, also placed in a point-to-point in 1984.
    Geeaway, placed third and fourth in I.N.H. flat races at four years, 1982; broodmare.

By Vulgan, out of **Skateaway**, won three races over fences including Conyngham Cup, Punchestown, and placed, including third in Galway Plate; dam of two winners from three foals, including Vulgaway (on the flat, over hurdles and fences; dam of two winners, including Shining Hour, on the flat, over hurdles and two races over fences, placed third in Northern Telecom Handicap Chase, **L**, and Like a Lord, placed on the flat, over hurdles and fences including second in P. Z. Mower Chase, **L**). By Foroughi, out of Zazzaway; dam of seven winners including Skateaway (see above), Jigaway (two races over fences), Skate Up (two races on the flat and six races under N.H. Rules), The Major (two races on the flat and 10 races under N.H. Rules), also Jazzaway (dam of **SPARKLING FLAME**, two races, also won three races over hurdles and six chases, including Galway Plate and Spa Hurdle, Cheltenham).

THE PROPERTY OF MR T. CLEGG

103
Non VAT

CHESNUT GELDING
1988

{ Buckskin (Fr.) { Yelapa { Mossborough
{ { { Your Point
{ { Bete a Bon Dieu { Herbager
{ { { Carraline
{ { Leander { Majority Blue
{ Rednael { { Westerlands Pearl
{ { New York { Flush Royal
{ { { Queen of the Dandies

This gelding has bee[n] ...
the owner is leaving ...
Sold with a Pre-Sale[s] ...

1st Dam
REDNAEL **won tw[o]** ...
Leeming Handicap ...
Breweries Novice ...
Dam of:
    Red Celtic (1 ...
    1988 c. by Bu ...

2nd Dam
NEW YORK wo[n] ...
Dam of **two winner[s]** ...
    NEW COLO[...]
    placed s ...
    Deep C[...]
        199 ...
    Rednael (se[e] ...
    Landing, p[...] ...

3rd Dam
QUEEN OF T[H]...
Dam of **three wi[nners]** ...
    DUKE OF [...]
        Guinn ...
        with a ...
    DOZO, se ...
        secon ...
    Langton [...]
        Colla[...]
        [...]
        Lang[...]
        Man[...]

New Yor[k] ...
Dandie [...] ...
    Prin[...] ...
    Wel[...] ...
    Our [...] ...

Her dam, M[...] ...
Toyette (wo[n] ...
flat and ove[r] ...

Doncaster Bloodstock Sales
Limited

AUGUST SALES

SUNDAY, 11th AUGUST — Show at 2.30 p.m.
MONDAY, 12th AUGUST — Sale at 10.00 a.m.
TUESDAY, 13th AUGUST — Sale at 10.00 a.m.

at t[...] S[...]
Tel[...]

Jack's entry in the Doncaster Sales catalogue,
from which he returned in disgrace having failed the vet

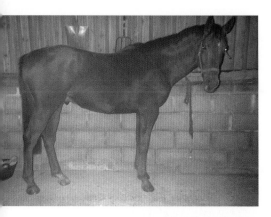

Jack as a four year old,
the day he came to stay
at Chris McGrann's

The start of Jack and
Jeanette's partnership

Back at the yard after this first trip to Scotland, and despite his legs being almost long enough to tie in a knot under Jack's belly, Jonty introduced Jack to competition, taking him *hors concours* round a charity one day event at Whixley Hall. Jonty also rode him in the Young Event Horse class at Bramham as a four year old – only to be slung out in the first round! "It wasn't that surprising," Fiona remembers. "The ring was full of fat four year olds and there was Jack looking very weedy, with his head in the air and Jonty's feet round his knees. I don't think Jonty was over impressed with the judges though!" That winter Jack had his first – and last – day's hunting with the Pendle Forest and Craven, the memory of which, according to Jeanette, is with him still. Whenever she saw the Duke of Beaufort's hounds on the horizon at Badminton, she would head Jack in the opposite direction before he decided to join them.

At the time Jeanette was based with Chris McGrann, who also gave lessons to Fiona Clegg on her regular event horse. Chris remembers that Jonty had had 'a misdemeanour' with Jack which left him concussed, and resulted in Fiona bringing Jack to the yard for a lesson.

Jeanette recalls it too. "It was in 1993, I remember that day really clearly. I was in the tack room and Fiona walked round the corner with her hand over her face. When she took it away I could see her cheek swelling up in front of my eyes. Jack had reared, whacked her in the face on the way up cracking her cheek bone, before going over backwards and depositing her on the ground.

It was the end of their relationship and the start of mine... Jack came to stay at Chris's." Fiona points out, "That's when it was Over To You, Jeanette!"

Chris took a lease on the horse from Tony Clegg, and Jeanette was the obvious jockey. "I'd seen Jeanette's talent from the start," Chris explains. "When she first came onto the yard I asked her what her ultimate ambition was: 'A Union Jack' she replied."

Jack was at the end of his fourth year when Jeanette took over the reins, and she started competing him as a five year old, when he was still owned by the Cleggs. After her accident Fiona admits that, "Never once when I saw Jack winning all over the world did I feel the slightest bit envious of Jeanette riding him!"

Luckily for Jeanette, Richard Holdsworth, a sponsor of Chris's and whose partner Lindsey Marsh had liveries with Chris, came up to the yard one day to watch Lindsey riding. Jeanette was schooling a coloured horse and she remembers, "I don't know exactly what it was, but he decided to back me. He said he'd buy me a horse, so I thought, 'well, Jack has been going all right, why not buy him?'"

"Chris had seen both Jeanette and Jack's potential," Lindsey explains. "Richard isn't horsey at all, but talking to Chris that day he decided, out of the blue, to support her. She and Jack just really gelled from the start. Richard now says that he always knew they would do well, but even he can't have imagined how well!"

Right: Mary Lett met up with Jack again at Tattersalls Horse Trials in June 2008, 20 years after selling him

14

Learning his trade

Jack pops round the Novice track at Henbury in 1994

According to Jeanette, Jack was always very sharp. "You'd be hacking down the road and he would whip round with no warning – not run off, but it was so quick. He could have just seen a plastic bag, but his main hates were, and still are, prams and dogs. Because of the way he moves, carrying his head and neck a bit high, he never used to take a contact, and with no real contact you didn't know what he was about to do, so he was always catching me out.

"Having said that, he was pretty good in competition, like he knew he had to behave. In our first few Pre Novices I'd almost been given some refusals, invariably because I'd not kicked hard enough and we'd had a dither at the edge of the water while he had a nosey at it. I remember getting back from one event and Chris saying 'if you let this horse stop I'm selling it'. So I pulled my finger out.

"Jack went up the grades quite easily once I got going," Jeanette remembers, "although I had no idea where he would take me then. I was only 18, and whilst I'd dreamt about riding at the Olympics from the age of eight, at the time all that was in my sights was the next event, or the goal for the year."

In their first season the pair contested five Pre Novices, winning two and never placed lower than eighth. They finished the year with two Novice runs, winning the first and placing second in the other. Toward the end of the following year Jack won his Intermediate section at Witton Castle, having also completed, and been placed in, his first three day event, the CCI* at Burgie.

"I finally left Chris's yard – or, perhaps more accurately, was pushed to leave, Chris quite rightly pointing out that

"He hasn't been a difficult horse to train at all. He's so elastic, and once he knew what was wanted of him he didn't find anything difficult."

17

Jack's first Intermediate run came at Clumber Park in 1994. He jumped double clear

it was about time I stood on my own two feet – when I was 20, four years after I had arrived. I went home to set up on my own, but despite having all the facilities I needed, I just didn't enjoy it. I hated having no-one to work with or to motivate me. Thank goodness, out of the blue Anne Marshall rang asking me to be the Lawrence David Event Team stable jockey. I jumped at the chance, it was a fantastic opportunity and enabled me to gain so much more experience with lots of different horses to ride. Of course, Jack went with me."

Anne Marshall was not impressed with Jack when he first arrived on her yard: "It was at the beginning of his career but when I saw him I thought 'Oh my god'. By the time Jeanette left, Jack had done his first Badminton."

At the time Jeanette was also competing Uncle Arthur (Prince), with whom she did both Juniors and Young Riders, but as she pointed out, "Prince had nothing like Jack's talent." In 1996, when Jack was eight, Jeanette took him to Bramham CCI***, the site of his less-than-successful foray into the Young Event Horse classes four years earlier. This time things were different, and Jeanette began to realise what a star she had.

She explains: "Early in the week Anne Marshall said to Lindsey 'Don't expect too much from your horse here'. That really got the bit between our teeth!" Lindsey agrees: "'We'll just see', I replied, hoping so much that Jack would prove Anne wrong." "We went out across country full of determination," Jeanette continues, "and he just ate it up – he found it very, very easy. He's always been a bold horse in that he never really backs off a fence. That's got him into trouble sometimes, but I've always known that whatever I point him at, the chances are, he'll jump it." The pair finished seventh, Jeanette and Lindsey's faith in Jack well placed.

"Having Jack with Jeanette has been wonderful from the start," Lindsey adds. "She has always only ever had Jack's best interests at heart. Richard and I respected the fact that she knew what she was doing, where he should run, how often he should run, when she should withdraw –

we could leave it all to her, knowing that he was in the best possible hands and any decisions would be made for the right reasons. As a rider, horse and owner team it worked perfectly for all of us."

A long standing pupil of Kenneth Clawson, whilst at the Marshall's Jeanette also received show jumping help from Mick and Andrew Saywell; in addition Jennie Lorriston-Clarke worked on Jack's flying changes. However, it was the year after their Bramham debut that Jeanette and Jack met the trainer who was to become one of the cornerstones of their success. John Bowen had started a training facility close to the Lawrence David stables and because Jeanette was having a few issues with her dressage she and Jack were sent along for some lessons.

'You don't see open corners like this much now. We were running in the novice at Jervaulx in 1994, Jack came fourth'

'This was at the Scottish Championships at Thirlestane Castle in 2002. Jack gave me a great ride, as usual'

20

'Not sure about the hat silks now, but I loved them at the time! This was taken at Chatsworth in 2000 where Jack placed seventh in the three star'

'I regularly used Belton as a main Badminton warm up. He jumped the novice track once, the intermediate once and the advanced nine times, almost always finishing in the top ten'

'Jack with John Bowen, who helped me to produce the best dressage tests that Jack was capable of at any stage in his career'

"The first time I met them I thought Jack looked like a very difficult horse to ride and train," John recalls. "He was conformationally challenged, but he was the ultimate athlete. He has everything in a horse that I love, complete articulation of his whole body. He wasn't the best mover, but everything did move – just not in the right direction. Because he wouldn't take a contact Jeanette didn't have control of all that energy, but I saw that despite this, as a rider she was a total natural. I remember ringing my soon-to-be wife and saying 'I have just taught the most amazing combination, they are going to hit the big time. There's just something about them.' Jeanette was like a sponge, absorbing information and striving to improve.

"The first thing Jeanette had to do was get a contact. It didn't matter how short Jack's neck went, or where his head went, until she had control of the reins she had no control of the energy. There has been a lot of controversy over the years about how I have trained Jeanette, teaching her to put Jack's neck really round and deep in order to get him to be a bit strong in the hand, because it's only when she has the connection that she can move his chin out to make the right shape.

"All through his career you have only had 10 minutes with him where he is right for the dressage. Over the years Jeanette and I developed a system that works, and fortunately, because of the great partnership we have built up, she trusts me to put her in absolutely the right place before she goes in to do an important test. She can then say 'OK, this is our 10 minutes'. I've seen her go around the outside of the arena at Badminton with Jack's nose between his knees in a completely incorrect outline, but as she makes the turn onto the centre line she lets his head come up and out and he performs the best test that he is capable of.

"Teaching him to take a contact has been the only barrier to his progress. My first impression was wrong – he hasn't been a difficult horse to train at all. He's so elastic, and once he knew what was wanted of him he didn't find anything difficult."

Jack, eager as ever to leave the start box, this time at Poplar Park in 2004

'This is at Belton again, in 2003. It must have been the perfect prep run that year because we went on to finish third at Badminton three weeks later'

'Jack's last run at Belton came in 2008 – and I galloped past one of the easiest fences on the Advanced track.

'I had watched the fence before the one I missed for a good 45 minutes because it was causing so many problems, and even watched horses gallop on and jump the one I didn't. Jack popped round as usual and I was delighted when we finished our round. It was only when I was riding back to the lorry park that a steward came up to me and said 'did you know that you missed a fence?' I thought he was winding me up!

'I was so cross with myself at the time but I saw the funny side eventually – I mean, how will I be able to sell him on as an eventer with an E on his record?'

Three day events

It was after their first CCI*** at Bramham in 1996 that Jeanette realised she might just have a four star horse. At the end of that season, bursting with confidence, they headed to Blenheim. Unfortunately things didn't quite go to plan. "I was a bit worried just before the event," Jeanette admits. "He felt like he was possibly throwing a splint but we arrived and he was OK – just not quite 100%. As usual he pinged around the cross country, coming home inside the time, but was very soon hopping lame. It turned out he had cracked his splint bone."

Jeanette was told by the on-site vet that he would have to have his splint bone taken out, "Well, there was no way that was happening!" Jack was taken to vet Andy Bathe who told Jeanette to give him six weeks box rest. It did the trick, and after that he was right as rain. Twelve months later Jeanette and Jack returned to Blenheim, finishing seventh.

"The only other time he was properly lame was the day after the World Games in Jerez. I took him to Andy again, once we got back to the UK, and he found a small bony growth, just under his coronet band. We rested him again and it went away."

This was the time when Ginny Leng (now Elliot) and Lucinda Green were bowing out of top level competition. Karen Dixon was still up there, but there was a definite lull before the likes of Leslie Law, William Fox-Pitt and Pippa Funnell took a hold on the team. As she prepared for her and Jack's first four star, Badminton, the following Spring, Jeanette knew that if they put up a good enough performance they were in with a shot of selection for the World Equestrian Games that autumn, in Pratoni del Vivaro, Italy.

"He was so naughty in the 10 minute box that we used to draw straws as to who had to grease his legs!"

"I was very, very nervous," Jeanette remembers, "petrified even! Jack coped brilliantly. I remember galloping through the finish thinking 'thank god for that!'" Lindsey Marsh had been no less nervous: "I walked the course and just thought, 'Oh my god!' I couldn't watch outside but stood in front of a screen so that I could turn away when I needed to!" Clear across country, Jack and Jeanette finished 16th and were on the shortlist, and later that year en route to Pratoni.

Their second Badminton appearance, in 1999, was just as testing as the first. Torrential rain on cross country day wreaked havoc with the field and Jeanette was no less apprehensive. John Bowen was with her and he remembers Joe, Jeanette's father, approaching him in the 10 minute box with a worried look on his face. "I knew I had to tell him Jeanette was going to run. Horse after horse had been falling. I had spoken to the British Chef d'Equipe, Giles Rowsell, about my concerns, to be told that the selectors thought the course rideable, but that riders should be sensible. Jeanette and Jack were on the Roads and Tracks section at the time.

"I'd been watching the action on the monitors as usual and could see that the lines we had planned simply weren't working; horses were slipping and falling. There was no

Badminton 2002. 'I love that fence and this sequence of photos. Jack is actually basculing over the jump! Unfortunately this was the year that Jack had his only horse fall at Badminton, later on in the course at Huntsman's Close'

way she could run on the lines that we had walked. When she came into the 10 minute box I sat her under a tree in the pouring rain, armed with a programme open at the pictures of the fences and a pen. Not with every fence, but with a lot of the influential ones I told her that she had to change her line. I literally drew on the pictures where she had to go. In typical Jeanette style she said, 'Fine, OK'. We went through it once, she got on and off she went, coming home clear. It was her second four star. I don't know how many riders you could do that with."

Joe Brakewell remembers it too. "May and I were terribly nervous. Every time Jeanette and Jack went cross country I would remind her just before she started to 'mind what you're doing'. We stood at the start and watched them jump the first. It was then a very long 12 minutes; each time the commentary said, 'and there's a run out for...' the gap before a name was given seemed like forever. It was definitely the most nerve wracking event for us; when we saw them come back over the last fence and through the finish we were totally physically and mentally drained. We went straight to the bar for a stiff drink!"

By 2000 the pair was established on the British Squad, so from then on plans were firmly centred around whatever championship was held in any given year.

Top left: 'I prefer to go early because I have nothing to influence me, I just ride the course as I walked it'

Left and opposite: 'The trot up and dressage pictures were taken in 2004, one of the wetter years! Jack finished seventh'

Above: 'Typical of Jack's jump; head high, and not necessarily the sharpest in front, but still scopey. This was 2003 when we had our best placing, finishing third'

Jeanette and Jack riding for home at Badminton in 2005, en route to fifth place

Jack's one fall at Badminton came in 2002, at the Huntsman's Close gate. Jeanette remembers: "It was late in the course and I was having a really good ride. Even when he took off I thought we were OK, but the next second we were flat on our sides. Jack leapt up, looked down at me and whinnied – I nearly cried!"

According to John Bowen, the fall was almost a foregone conclusion. "We'd walked that line a hundred times together. I don't train Jeanette for jumping, but we always walked big courses together – although the further she went in her career, rightly the less influence I had. Every time we walked Huntsman's Close she started her turn a bit early. I would grab her by the coat and say 'not yet'. She has such a natural eye, which is what's good about her, but it led her to make that mistake. But there are times when you can't stop things and Jeanette paid a harsh penalty for a very minor error that she might have got away with another day."

However Jack retained his place on the British team despite this, and the following year posted his best four star placing, again at Badminton, when he was the only

'Jack has just been so consistent when competing at Badminton, in all three phases'

horse to finish on his dressage score. "Finishing third in 2003 was a real highlight for me," Jeanette confesses. "In part that was because of outside pressure I was under at the time – it was just a massive relief to get through the week and finish with a good result."

Jack might have been a model event horse when in action, but he wasn't always the easiest horse to care for, as groom David (Davina) Edney remembers. "I always dreaded washing him off in the 10 minute box at a three day event! The minute you put water on him he was off, reversing at high speed. Badminton 2003 was the worst, he bucked his rug off twice and was ploughing backwards as we tried to get him ready. Jeanette was sitting on her seat trying to ignore him and focus on the course when she finally had enough, leapt to her feet and smacked him really hard. So he *must* have been behaving badly! He was so naughty in the 10 minute box that we used to draw straws as to who had to grease his legs!"

Catherine Cawdron, who also groomed for Jack, agrees: "Jack was always a monkey to do at Badminton. I'm sure he thought that all the crowds had come just to see him. All bar one year, in fact the year he fell, he was stabled in the Portcullis yard, which is outside the main stabling complex. It's a quiet yard of about 14 boxes and Jack could always see out, which he loves. The main excitement came when it was time for the daily exercise of the Duke of Beaufort's hounds. Jack was always more than keen to go and join them!

"Tying him up was never an option which made washing off quite interesting – but given he's so athletic with his hind legs it's pretty amazing that he only managed to kick me once, when I was putting his cross country grease on."

'I remember the first time I rode down to the Badminton Lake. I was nervous as hell! I'd only been there once and then watched it on TV. After that first year though all the negative thoughts were put to bed, Jack knew where he was and what he had to do'

By 2004 Jack was really making Badminton his own. That year he finished seventh, in 2005 he was fifth and in 2006 fourth – rolling just one show jump in three appearances.

Despite this, 2006 was the year when the British Selectors decided that his team days were over. With no World Games to prepare for, Jeanette took Jack to his very first Burghley CCI****, at the grand old age of 18. "I thought the course would really suit him – possibly more so even than Badminton because of the hills. He had been there once before when we rode the guinea pig dressage test in 2001, but it was great to take him round the cross country."

Just as they had done at their first Bramham ten years earlier, Jeanette and Jack silenced any doubters by romping round the cross country track, clear inside the time, to finish seventh. Those who felt that he should have been at the World Games in Aachen that summer were vindicated. For John Bowen it was one of his fondest memories. "That was special. It's a different type of course and track, and for Jack to make it appear as effortless as he has always made Badminton – or anywhere else – look was amazing. He skipped round as if it were a Pony Club course."

His final three day appearance came at Badminton in 2007. It wasn't an easy decision for Jeanette. "I was really disappointed the previous year when he had finished fourth there but still not been selected for the team – what more did he have to do? I genuinely felt he could have posted a counting score in Aachen. Given that his team days were over he had nothing more to prove, but he was fit and well so deserved one last big run".

True to form Jack put in a proficient dressage performance and beat the clock home after a foot perfect cross country round. A single rail down in the final phase dropped the pair to 14th.

Badminton 2006. Jack again jumped a double clear, finishing on his dressage score in fourth place

'Leaving a leg is something Jack occasionally did, but this was the first time he did it jumping into water. Luckily we got away with it'

'This was a very special occasion. Burghley has always been one of my favourite three day events, so to be able to take Jack there in 2006 was great. It was good to fit it into his career record'

Jack performed a good dressage test at Burghley, although the American judge Marilyn Payne was less impressed than her fellow judges. She gave Jack a mark of 174, Italy's Giulio Pocci was more generous with 190 while Jennie Lorriston-Clarke awarded him 191

Burghley 2006. Jack jumped a clear round across country, inside the time as usual

'I was really cross about our two fences down at Burghley. I think I probably tried too hard because it was always going to be Jack's only ever run there. I worked him in for too long in the collecting ring. Even worse, one down would have left us fourth and a few thousand pounds better off!'

'The last time Jack jumped the Vicarage Vee was in 2007. This photo shows how accurate you had to be to jump it. There isn't a lot of room, and if you make a mistake it's a very deep ditch'

Jeanette recalls how she felt throughout that week. "It was really difficult because I knew that everything we did was going to be Jack's last. I don't think he had a clue, but I blubbed my eyes out before we went into the main arena on the Sunday! You have to stop at some point though. He's still not really got any wear and tear on him and he trots up sound, but he is beginning to show the first inevitable signs of a bit of stiffness."

Everyone involved with Jack's career seems to have their own special memories from that final Badminton. For Catherine Cawdron it was, "the saddest day, but what an amazing achievement. It won't be the same without him."

John Bowen was, "fine until Jack went into the main arena for his last dressage test. I was ready for the actual announcement on the Sunday, but I hadn't prepared myself for how I might feel when I realised that I had done my last warming up session with him."

Giles Rowsell was commentating at the trot up: "There was Jack, standing in front of the Ground Jury, with legs that looked like they should be on a six year old starting out, not a 19 year old coming to the end of his career. It just shows what you can achieve with a well put together horse that is properly managed."

"It was really difficult because I knew that

everything we did was going to be Jack's last.

I don't think he had a clue, but I blubbed my

eyes out before we went into the main arena

on the Sunday!"

Flying the flag

After their performance at their first Badminton in 1998 the pressure was on. Jeanette remembers: "Things were done differently then and there was a final trial before selection was made for the World Games at Pratoni del Vivaro. That year it was at Henbury Horse Trials in Cheshire. Everyone on the short list was competing and we all stabled together nearby. Trot up was the morning after the event. Only then did the Selectors name the squad."

According to Giles Rowsell, the Chef d'Equipe, that year a large number of horses had dropped out of contention through injury. "We had already earmarked Jeanette as a real rider for the future. She showed her ability at Young Rider level, but had never had a good enough horse to make the team. With Jack it was obvious they were going to become a formidable partnership, although I don't think any of us realised then quite how good they would be."

"It was an unforgettable moment for Jeanette's parents Joe and May when Giles handed Jeanette her Union Jack."

'This was at the Henbury final trial. I knew we had a good chance of selection if all went well, so just gave it my best shot'

'Our first medal, team gold at Luhmühlen. The team that year were Ian Stark, Pippa Funnell, Tina Gifford (now Cook) and me'

It was an unforgettable moment for Jeanette's parents Joe and May when Giles handed Jeanette her Union Jack. "It was such a defining moment," says Joe. "We had always believed that Jeanette and Jack would represent Great Britain, and we were unbelievably proud of them both."

Jeanette was chosen to ride as an individual at Pratoni, admitting with hindsight that this was a good thing. "Jack had what was probably his first ever proper refusal. About two thirds of the way round the course you galloped to the top of a hill, jumped two steps down and then had two forward strides to a curving wave fence. It was the only fence I was worried about – which is exactly why he stopped! I was indecisive, and he didn't know what to do because in those days I used to give him quite a lot of input on the cross country. Instead of kicking him off the steps I just let him drop down and we reached the final element on two and a half strides. Basically I was inexperienced and didn't make the right decision – but we learnt from it."

A year later the pair was promoted to the British team, and took what was to become their regular role as pathfinders at the European Championships in Luhmühlen. Team training at Badminton just prior to their departure had provoked one worrying moment when Jack showed signs of colicing. The stable yard was very busy and Jack was becoming unsettled, so John Bowen took matters into his own hands and sent groom Fraser Kirby out into the Park with Jack, with strict instructions to 'keep him walking and don't come back for hours'. It did the trick.

"I like to go first for a team because I don't have any input from other riders; I can just ride off what I see. Back then it seemed quite daunting though, and my lasting memory from Luhmühlen is of setting off to the roads and tracks in the near dark and fog, barely able to see in front of Jack's nose. I must have been a bit nervous because I also remember asking Mandy Stibbe if she had any Lipsyl when I saw her at the start of phase A! She gave me loads of confidence, reminding me that we were there for a reason."

'Jack's owners Richard & Lindsey came out to support us at Luhmühlen, which was great'

'En route to Sydney. Catherine had to spend hours making sure that everything was spotless in case we were checked on arrival – we weren't but it was better to play safe'

'I was concerned about the length of time Jack was going to be on the plane. There had been talk of horses getting travel sickness on long journeys because they had to keep their heads up for so long, but he travelled well'

'We spent some time in quarantine at Waresley before we left. A man in a white coat arrived from Defra to spray the horses with something, but he can't have got the dosage right. I'd gone into Newmarket to do some shopping, and Catherine rang me saying Jack was in a state, kicking out and coming up in a rash. He kicked both of his back shoes off! Fortunately it didn't last long'

Right: 'It's really nice to have such support from home, especially when you are so far away'

Sydney Olympics 2000. 'I loved this fence. It was very straightforward, but had been so beautifully painted – the amount of effort that had gone into it epitomised the care taken with the whole event. I had to jump into the ditch to get a close up look!'

These photos, and the ones overleaf, were all taken at Sydney

'I thought events were better with roads and tracks when Jack was younger, but he probably grew out of it, so the timing worked well for him. One good thing with short format is that there is no 10 minute box so there was less mutiny with the grease!'

'I didn't get the best shot into this fence...'

"Sydney was different from anywhere I had been before. I had wanted to ride at an Olympics since I was eight, so to be there was almost unbelievable."

"We were running after Ireland's Ginny McGrath and The Yellow Earl, who was first out and who apparently walked all over the first fence on the steeplechase. The fences were more like banks with a bit of brush on the top than what we used to see in Britain, so there was no opportunity to be half hearted. With Mandy's words still in my ears we really set out to attack it.

"The cross country course itself was pretty decent. I'd been undecided whether to go long or straight at the first water which came up very early, but I heard over the tannoy that Ginny had had a problem so took the safer option. Then there was a complex about half way round that had a very square front profiled final element. I hate fences like that – but I needn't have worried, Jack was great."

Catherine Cawdron groomed for Jeanette for all bar one of her team appearances, starting with Luhmühlen. "I remember being quite nervous. Because Jeanette was first to go for the team it was an early start on cross country day. There were no lights in the stables so plaiting was a nightmare, and there was barely enough daylight to jump the steeplechase fences. I was so relieved when they came home clear."

Great Britain won gold, with Jeanette and Jack finishing in ninth place having established their role within the team. The next goal was the Sydney Olympics in 2000.

"Sydney was different from anywhere I had been before. I had wanted to ride at an Olympics since I was eight, so to be there was almost unbelievable.

"We were the fourth team in; the Australians were the third, so I followed Andrew Hoy into the dressage arena. I made sure we kept well out of the way until the crowd had finished cheering his test – Jack wouldn't have appreciated that! Again the cross country was decent enough. The fences were pretty big and there were lots of places to gallop on and make up time. Once the first water was out of the way I started to enjoy it. It was at the second water, though, that Jack was really clever. I've seen it on video and watched it in slow motion and I still can't really believe it. We jumped in over a log, and then it was followed by three or four strides to a jump up onto an island, then a bounce back into the water. Jack jumped up onto the bank, took off with his front end to tackle the bounce and then literally shuffled his hind legs forward to get a bit closer before taking off.

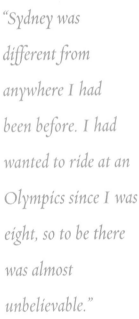

"Initially the team was disappointed to win silver, knowing that they had been within reach of gold, but soon realised it was a great result."

59

He just amazes me! That was so clever of him. In hindsight that was one of the best rounds he ever jumped, he took every fence just as I had imagined and didn't put a single foot wrong."

Catherine Cawdron doesn't totally agree about the not putting a foot wrong in Sydney: "We had to have his stable rebuilt twice because he kept kicking holes in the back of it!"

Jeanette admits that initially the team was disappointed to win silver, knowing that they had been within reach of gold. "That morning we had got up early to watch the coxless four win gold, after which we were really

European Team Gold number two. The team in Pau were Leslie Law, Pippa Funnell, William Fox-Pitt and Jeanette

'The next element of this was a real 'Jack leave a leg fence' so I remember helping him quite a lot here!'

"Even the figure of eight steeplechase track was tough to ride because of the constant turning."

'Me in my trolley dolly uniform, standard issue for Jerez!'

fired up to do the same – but at the end of the day, the Aussies had as many down as we did. We soon realised we were being a bit spoilt to be disappointed and were delighted with the result, particularly given that it was both my and Pippa Funnell's first Olympics." Jack again placed ninth.

The second European team gold medal came at Pau in 2001, Jack finishing just out of the top 10. "I remember Pau being a fairly twisty track so you had to keep your foot to the floor the whole way to get the time. I came home thinking we'd jumped a nice but not brilliant round, but apparently Yogi Breisner (British team coach) still uses the tape of it when giving talks to demonstrate how a cross country round should be ridden. Good old Jack!"

'This is one of my favourite pictures, taken at Jerez. It's a big fence and Jack makes it look so easy'

'It's a testament to Jack's athleticism, and the fact that he is a thoroughbred, that he came out after such a tough cross country day in Jerez and show jumped so well'

For Jeanette, her proudest moment with Jack came at the 2002 World Equestrian Games in Jerez de la Frontera, Spain, where the team won bronze and Jeanette took the Individual Silver medal. "It was a total surprise to get an individual medal – no-one expected it, least of all me! I could say it was due to other riders misfortunes, but that's the sport. The cross country track was the toughest I have ever jumped – the ground was pretty firm and it was very twisty and therefore hard to get into a rhythm. I felt that after every fence I had to really gallop to try and make up time. Even the figure of eight steeplechase track was tough to ride because of the constant turning, but I was luckier than some in that Jack's pretty manoeuvrable and very light on his feet. Lots of good

horses had problems. Both William (Fox-Pitt) and Pippa (Funnell) had stops, and Leslie (Law) crossed his tracks. The fact that the team still won bronze shows how many problems the other teams had too."

Jeanette and Jack were in sixth place going into the show jumping. Jack rolled a pole for four penalties. Then one by one those above her rolled more. "I still wouldn't have won if we'd jumped clear because the overnight leader, Jean Teulère, jumped clear, thoroughly deserving his gold medal."

Jerez was the one Championship where Davina Edney groomed for Jeanette. "I look back at 2002 as the most

"Jack is a little Barry McGuigan.

He's obliging, reliable and very, very tough."

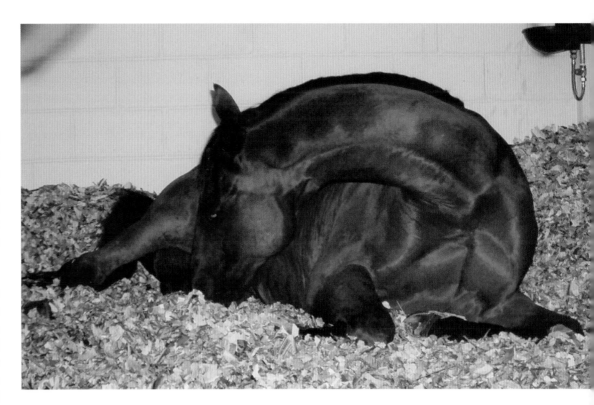

incredible year of my life. Jeanette finished eighth and ninth at Burghley on other rides, and we went straight on to Jerez. It was the first time that I had flown with horses so I was pretty nervous, and while we were driving down the A14 we came across Blyth Tait whose lorry had broken down. So, in the middle of the night we loaded Ready Teddy onto our lorry; fortunately the road wasn't too busy!

"Everyone knows Jack isn't a dressage horse, but it was always expected that Jeanette would go out first for the team, jump clear inside the time across country – and probably have one rail down in the show jumping. That's just how it was. I knew it was a tough course and the pressure was pretty intense. Before the show jumping a medal of any sort, team or individual, seemed unlikely. The team were in fourth and Jack was lying sixth. Lots of people were having rails though and suddenly it looked like the team might scrape a medal, so I was sent back to the stables to get everyone's smart hats and white bandages for the horses.

"I missed Jack's climb up the leaderboard completely! When I got back everyone in the British camp was jumping around in huge excitement. I asked Jeanette what had happened and she said, "Silver… and team bronze" – it didn't sink in. It was only when the team show jump coach Kenneth Clawson came over, gave me a hug and said, 'Well done, you really deserve this,' that the penny dropped. I just burst into tears! Jack knew he was the star, he loved the attention. Nothing will ever top that – it was the end of an amazing three weeks."

The only blot on Jack's British team record came at the 2003 European Championships, held at Punchestown. It was the only time Jeanette and Jack weren't the pathfinders for the team, and they fell at the final water.

'Our one fall when representing Britain was at Punchestown. Jack was jumping so well until this point and I just made a big boo-boo. Funnily enough it was the only fence that I hadn't been able to visualise how it would jump'

"It was one of those fences; you didn't really know what was going to happen," Jeanette explains. "Jack can get quite complacent later on in a course, he just gallops and jumps and doesn't really back off his fences unless they are big. I didn't get the right stride – I should probably have just sat there and kicked, but because the fence on the island had a boxy profile and it was near the end of the course I was worried he might be a bit blasé. I think his head was a bit high and he got too deep to the bottom of the step up, hit it with his forearm and we both hit the deck. Just like when he fell at Badminton he leapt to his feet, looked down and whinnied at me. Because it was a horse fall we were eliminated."

Lindsey Marsh had been standing at the water, and Jack fell right in front of her. "I think my heart stopped beating! I was so relieved to see them both back on their feet, though Jack didn't look over-impressed."

The pair was still on the plane to the Olympic Games in Athens in 2004. "Athens was completely different to Sydney," Jeanette remembers. "It wasn't a big course, the only decent question was the water." It was the first year that eventing had run short format with no steeplechase or roads and tracks, and there had been concerns about the heat and humidity in Greece. On the day it wasn't a problem and the horses finished as fresh as anything, although according to Catherine Cawdron Jack was still keen to sample the de-misting tents. Unfortunately for the British it was more of a dressage and show jumping competition because so many riders jumped clear across country. Nevertheless another medal, initially team bronze but later team silver, made its way to Jeanette's home.

Perhaps appropriately Jack's final team performance came on British soil, at the 2005 Blenheim European

66

Championships. Home inside the time across country and with just one show jump down the 17 year old Jack was showing no signs of ageing. "I went early on, before the downpour. Would I have stayed in the plate in the conditions Zara (Phillips) experienced? Who knows? When your saddle is that wet it is really slippery... she was phenomenal. Expectations were high because we had a really solid team (Zara, William Fox-Pitt, Leslie Law and Jeanette) and we were all expected to jump clear – fortunately we did. The crowds were amazing, at least 90% of them cheering for the Brits. It was absolutely fantastic – and Jack loves a crowd!" The team didn't disappoint, and the sixth consecutive European team gold medal went to Britain.

Looking back at the many Championships Jack has taken Jeanette to she is adamant that, "they were all really special, but I wouldn't mind forgetting my fall in Punchestown. Jerez has to stand out because our individual medal was so unexpected. I'll never forget standing with Kenneth Clawson watching those above me. One came out and Kenneth said 'you're fifth now', then 'you're fourth now', then it was bronze – and finally silver. Kenneth, who I have trained with for years, was in tears, I was in tears, and it was really emotional."

Kenneth agrees: "Being pathfinder invariably means that you sacrifice any chance of an individual medal – Thursday morning dressage marking is never the highest! For the pair of them to win individual silver was very, very special, and a hugely emotional moment for all of us."

Jeanette adds: "I feel incredibly honoured to have had a partner like Jack who has taken me to places that even I never dreamt of."

'We were early to go in Athens and there weren't many people in the stands. I had to follow Bettina Hoy, which wasn't ideal, but Jack did a good test'

Opposite: 'I was very surprised that Jack liked the misting fans. I thought he would stand on the edge and refuse to go in, but Catherine said that he loved them'

'This was the only fence where I wasn't sure what would happen, but Jack popped through it and made it feel easy'

'The cake at our farewell supper before we left for Athens'

'Shame about the white legs!'

An Aussie wearing a Team GB shirt! Brook (Staples) knew which rider he should be supporting!

Lindsey Marsh and Richard Holdsworth's daughter Lucy went out to Athens to cheer on Jeanette and Jack

'Jack's last team appearance, Blenheim 2005 – but it was great to have it on home ground with the crowd behind us. Although I hoped it wouldn't be our last Championship I half thought it might be. The team were Leslie Law, Zara Phillips, William Fox-Pitt and me'

Jack was in 10th place after the dressage phase at Blenheim

'Jack never cooled down that quickly after cross country because of the excitement around the start and finish. Because he was around for so long the vets all got to know him really well so we were allowed to take him back to the stable to relax'

'John (Bowen) was watching our round on the screen in the 10 minute box. As we set out he overheard one Frenchman say to his friend: "Watch this, this is a unique horse"'

After a clear cross country round inside the time, Jack rolled one show jump pole to finish 12th individually

'In hindsight it was in with the new (Zara) and out with the old (Leslie and me), but Blenheim was a great way for Jack to finish his role as a team member'

Right: Playing up to the photographers

A legend retires

Over To You has undoubtedly been the horse of a lifetime for Jeanette. Gifted to her by Richard Holdsworth in 2006 Jack will live out his days on her Derbyshire yard. "It was the right thing to do," according to Richard. "He has been part of her daily life for so long, it wouldn't be fair to take him away." Mark Johnson, a long time owner of Jeanette's and follower of Jack's, went into partnership with Jeanette to fund his running costs. "I jumped at the chance when Jan rang me; who wouldn't?" he admits, before pointing out, "she didn't really need me though – Jack more than covered his costs in prize money that first year!"

Jack retired from three day eventing in 2007 but continued to show a swift turn of foot at one day events in 2008, consistently jumping clear across country. Now, however, Jeanette has decided his eventing days must come to an end.

Jack is still hugely popular with the public, undisputedly prompting the biggest cheers in the Eventers Grand Prix class at Blenheim 2007, with applause for every fence he jumped. He inspired another standing ovation at the NEC the following Spring when he tried his hand at the British Indoor Cross Country.

"I was working him in the collecting ring," Jeanette smiles, "and the stewards opened the big curtains to let one horse out and another in to the arena. He saw the lights and heard the applause, his ears pricked up and he just knew what was coming. I've no doubt he thought everyone was there just to see him!" At his final Chatsworth Horse Trials appearance spectators flocked to the dressage to watch Jack, and the crowds were clapping on the cross country before he even reached a fence.

"The thing is, he's not really Jeanette's horse, he's everybody's. Everybody knows him and everybody loves him."

Jack jumping double clear in the Burnham Market World Cup qualifier, March 2008

"I don't think he's going to be that happy about retirement, but he's not a horse that could go back and compete at a lower level like so many do. For a start I would never let anyone else compete him, however selfish that might sound," Jeanette admits. "Maybe he'll do the odd novelty class, like the Hickstead Eventers Grand Prix, if he's feeling really well, but he won't be registered with British Eventing again. He'll just tick over at home, I'll hack him out as will Sambo, my head girl."

Sambo (Samantha Hobbs) has no problems with that, she clearly adores Jack. "I will never forget the first time I rode him – I thought all my Christmases had come at once! It was totally unexpected and happened out of the blue. Jeanette was going away the following week and she legged me up saying 'you'd better learn to ride him before I go'. I must have rung every single person I know that evening to tell them what I'd done! It felt a bit like sitting on a giraffe at first, and I was amazed that he is really quite lazy – how Jeanette makes it look so effortless is beyond me.

"I'm surely one of the luckiest people in the country because I get to ride Jack on the gallops, while Jeanette rides the really naughty horses. He's like a Ferrari; he just floats along with me dreaming that I'm galloping up towards the Lake at Badminton…"

Jeanette adds, "He doesn't have the end stable in the yard because he doesn't like to be on his own even though he is incredibly independent. He's always been a bit grumpy, and I'm sure he's getting grumpier with age. He hates his tummy being groomed, and if I go to trim his feathers you'd think I was trying to pull a scab off him. He scowls and fights and isn't a horse that likes being patted – but if you have Polos in your pocket he's your best mate!"

Left: Jeanette and Sambo get Jack ready for the show jumping at the Chatsworth World Cup qualifier, May 2008

Right: Also at Chatsworth, Jack posts another cross country clear to huge applause from the crowds

"He scowls and fights and isn't a horse that likes being patted — but if you have Polos in your pocket he's your best mate!"

Washing off has never been Jack's favourite bit, but he's got softer about it as he's got older

But Sambo counters, "He's grumpy with Jeanette because she makes him work! He's much softer with the rest of us, and he'll even have a cuddle in the stable sometimes – when Jeanette isn't looking!"

Catherine Cawdron hasn't worked full time for Jeanette since 2000 but still feels like she knows Jack inside out. "He doesn't like being pampered and can pull a good face – but that's as far as he would go. He's a very private horse who doesn't like fuss, unless it's the applause that he so often provokes – he'll take any amount of that!"

Davina Edney worked for Jeanette for four years. He admitted: "It's weird looking back – I only realise now how amazing Jack was when I was looking after him. At the time I knew he was good, but not how good. I'll never forget the first time I met him. Jeanette walked up to his stable with me and said 'This is the good horse'. I looked in and there he was, a small, upside down chestnut, standing at the back of his stable, weaving. I thought, 'Oh, OK…!'

"When I came back and worked with him at Burnham Market in his final season he was a different horse – a real joy to handle. I couldn't believe how chilled out he's become. I'll never work with another horse like him, I'm sure of that."

Davina summed it up when he said, "the thing is, he's not really Jeanette's horse, he's everybody's. Everybody knows him and everybody loves him."

"We are so enormously proud of Jack," Lindsey Marsh admits. "My biggest regret is that I didn't go to the Sydney Olympics. Watching him on the television Richard and I finally realised quite how good he was. It was an incredible feeling to own a horse that was representing Great Britain – and doing it so well."

May Brakewell, Jeanette's mother, is equally proud. "I will never forget standing at the water fence in Sydney and watching Jack jump through, foot perfect.

Davina came back to help at Burnham Market – he got quite emotional seeing Jack again

We didn't see him again until he was galloping along the skyline towards the last fence, inside the time and clear all the way. That will stay with me forever."

How do you decide to retire a horse like Over To You? "God knows," was Jeanette's answer. "I just feel now, not that he's hard work to ride at home but that he gets bored. Let's face it, he's been in work for 15 years, so it's not surprising that he doesn't have quite the same enthusiasm he used to. He has still loved competing, running across country with his ears pricked, full of life, but at home he feels an older horse. It's a difficult one. I think you can keep going, but you don't want a bad day to determine the stopping time. He's got nothing to prove. He might not have won masses, but he has been so consistent and is always there or thereabouts."

With four European Team Gold medals, two Olympic Team Silvers, one World Team Bronze, not forgetting his individual World Silver medal, Jack has entered the record books as the most medalled event horse in history. His British Eventing points total, which stands at over 2150, will quite probably never be bettered. Eventing just won't be quite the same without him.

"You don't want a
bad day to determine
the stopping time.
He's got nothing
to prove."

'Jack will stay at home, ticking over to maintain his condition. He'd hate to be completely retired and put in a field, so he'll make the odd appearance. He'll let me know what he wants to do'

Jack with Sambo,
Jeanette's head girl

Pages from Jack's passport, which was officially marked
'FULL' at his final overseas event, Tattersalls 2008

Jack with Jeanette and
Mark Johnson

Testimonials

Jeanette Brakewell: Why did I want to do a book about Jack? He deserves it.

Joe Brakewell, Jeanette's father: Eventing must be the only sport that is better afterwards than during, if you're watching. May and I would get terribly nervous – May from a week before the event! My nerves started when Jeanette rode into the start box and lasted until she crossed the finish line. We knew that Jeanette felt there was nothing Jack couldn't jump though. I'll never forget standing in front of the scoreboards at the World Equestrian Games in Jerez and hearing so many people saying Jeanette's name in so many languages; it was the strangest feeling and a very proud moment.

May Brakewell, Jeanette's mother: I would like to thank Richard for buying Jack all those years ago, and Lindsey for no doubt asking him; but mostly for keeping Jack with Jeanette throughout his career. The memory of them both galloping along the skyline towards the last fence in Sydney, inside the time and clear all the way will stay with me forever.

Lindsey Marsh, owner for most of Jack's life: Richard and I are so proud to have owned Jack and been a part of his extraordinary life. It's been a fabulous journey.

Mark Johnson, co-owner with Jeanette: Jack is unique, an amazing character and a lovely person. He wouldn't hurt a fly, but you never quite know what he's going to do next. I've followed his career for years, and when I had the chance of being part of his story, I jumped at it.

Pippa Funnell, British team member: Jack is unique, and together he and Jeanette made an exceptional partnership. As part of the team we knew we could rely on them; even in the dressage which wasn't Jack's strongest phase he was totally consistent. He might not have had the biggest movement but he was light on his feet and correct. Invariably going first across country he would give us all so much confidence. We knew after his round that any course could be jumped; we always started on a good note.

William Fox-Pitt, British team member: Jack's record speaks for itself; both at the big events at home and at Championships his performance has been second to none. It shows his ability, resilience and enjoyment of the sport and exemplifies Jeanette's training and horse management that she has kept him going, fit and sound, for so long.

Jonty Evans, who backed Jack: I knew Jack was talented but never expected him to be as successful as he has been. It's been great to watch him with Jeanette over the years. I'm just proud to have been part of his life – he really is the most inquisitive, bright horse you could ever find.

Fiona Saxby, whose father bought Jack as a two year old: What a privilege to have been part of his early life. I've loved watching his success and think he found his own luck by failing the vet at Doncaster as a youngster, thereby meeting Jeanette.

John Bowen, Jeanette and Jack's dressage trainer: Jack is a testament to Jeanette's management and riding. To retire, sound and competitive, at 20 is rare. People say Jeanette is lucky to have had him; luck has had nothing to do with it. She has managed Jack's career from day one. She has never run him inside the time or pushed him at a one day event unnecessarily. Everything has been about keeping his technique and his jumping right, keeping his soundness right. He has only ever been really competitive at three day events. I don't think there will ever be another horse like him.

Kenneth Clawson, British team show jump trainer: I have watched Jack at every single three day event that he has done, from 2* level upwards. He and Jeanette were just such a powerful combination, such fighters. To me Jack is a little Barry McGuigan. He's obliging, reliable and very, very tough.

Giles Rowsell, Jeanette's first Chef d'Equipe: The partnership of Jeanette and Jack has been tremendously influential to Britain's success. He is a very talented jumper, she is a very talented rider.

Catherine Cawdron, groom to Jack at most of his big events: I feel extremely honoured to have looked after the world's most outstanding event horse, Over To You. The memories will be with me forever.

Samantha Hobbs, Jeanette's current head girl: There will never be another Jack, he is totally unique.

Jenny Hall, British team vet: Jack has been a fantastic servant to the British team, he's a truly amazing horse. When I first saw him, I wasn't sure. He's not the most impressive when he trots up in a straight line, but trot him on a circle on hard ground and he's sound as a bell. We x-rayed him not that long ago and his legs were still really clean; he's such a resilient horse. Interestingly his bloods were rarely 'normal'. It shows that you have to look at the horse as a whole, these things don't necessarily mean that they can't perform at the highest level.

Pippa Roome, Eventing Editor, Horse & Hound: Everyone with an interest in eventing in this country owes so much to Over To You – just think how many medals might have slipped through Britain's fingers without him. It's been a privilege to choose pictures of him to use in the magazine and follow the final part of his career so closely since I joined H&H. At the Blenheim Europeans, I remember thinking how lucky we were to have a pathfinder you could watch going across country with such total confidence. I also loved seeing him at his final Badminton in 2007 – he obviously knew exactly where he was and what he needed to do.

Mike Tucker, course designer and commentator: My lasting memory of Jack is from Jerez, where I had designed the cross country course. Thousands had been spent on the going in advance of the cross country, but then the watering was stopped a week before the event and the sun baked the ground. Whilst other horses faltered Jeanette and Jack were outstanding. They jumped all the routes as I wanted them jumped. From that moment he has always had a special corner in my heart.

Alan Smith, Daily Telegraph: For sheer, top-level consistency there will probably never be another horse like him. Leading the way for the British team he and Jeanette could always be relied on to do a great job. Eight consecutive Championship medals is testament to their collective reliability – and the individual silver at the World Championships in Jerez showed that they could do it alone as well.

Anne Lawrence, Lawrence Marshall event team: What Jack went on to achieve was phenomenal. Having known him at the start of his career I was amazed, especially how he coped with the huge amount of travelling – I remember him kicking my lorry to pieces!

From Jack's followers

Laura Penny: I will most remember Over To You for his many great cross country rounds and the fantastic job he done as pathfinder for the British team. How lucky we have been to have on our side such an amazing horse who, ears pricked, popped round the toughest of courses. His record of World, Olympic and European medals is outstanding for any sport.

Ian White: Watching Jeanette and Jack across country was always an inspiration. In 2003 I went on a course walk around Burghley with Jeanette. That was when I decided to start eventing myself. I aspire to ride as well as her. My goal is to have my horse, Moose make cross country courses look as easy as Jack does.

Kelly Hibbitt: My proudest moment came when I found out that my little ex-racehorse turned event horse is related to Jack through their grandsire, Riverman. I saw Jack in his stable at Barbury Castle and, other than his colouring, he resembled my Dougal uncannily!

Margaret and Stewart Golder: We were in Jerez at the World Equestrian Games. Jack's dressage was one of his best, followed by a clear across country. On show jumping day we took our seats in the stadium, with Jeanette's parents on either side of us. Jeanette was in sixth place when Jack had one jump down... my husband was calculating the scores quicker than the commentator as each successive rider's penalties put Jeanette up a place. May and Joe couldn't watch: thank goodness we had the video camera!

Helen Camfield: I've always enjoyed watching Jack compete. He's a wonderful example of a 'non-conventional' eventer. Everyone loves to imagine what it would be like to ride these wonderful Badminton-bound eventers across country – Jack just looked like so much fun. The sort of horse you had to smile at. I go to Badminton every year and have been privileged to see Jack jump round on a number of occasions. The time I will always remember though was his last run there. He and Jeanette oozed enjoyment and enthusiasm. To me Badminton is the lesser without Jack's participation. I missed him this year.

Fiona Lewis: Jack first caught my eye when I was watching the Olympic Games in 2000. I was just 8 and he reminded me so much of my little 13 hand pony, Jester. How similar they look and behave too; liver chestnut, fine-boned, wiry, very handsome, full-of-life, cheeky, but all heart, and like Jack, Jester's passion has always been jumping and he puts up with the dressage knowing that something much more exciting comes next! Every time I see Jester I think of Jack – a miniature version and he's even the same age.

Laura Humphreys: Over To You is self-assured, confident, and with a tenacious streak that I think has certainly contributed to his astonishing competition record and his seemingly effortless soundness. His departure from competition will leave a small but significant hole in the eventing world. My lasting memory is of a chestnut horse who jumped as easily as he breathed, but one who when cuddled by Jeanette on his retirement, pulled the most perfect, "Get off Mum!" face I've ever seen. That sums him up for me, he knows how great he is, and frankly, who's going to disagree?

Jack jumping into the water at the 2006 British Open Championships at Gatcombe Park

92

Chronology

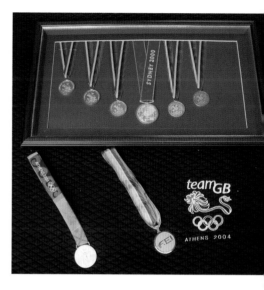

1988	Born in County Wexford, Ireland, six months later sold to Tom Costello
1990	Bought by Tony Clegg, shipped to England
1991	Sent to Tom Tate's racing yard
1991 Aug	Failed the vet at Doncaster Sales, returned to the Clegg's
1992	Taken to The Royal (Dick) Veterinary Centre for the first time
1993	'Over to you Jeanette' – Jeanette gets the ride on Jack
1993 April	Jack does his first affiliated event, a Pre Novice at Witton Castle
1993 May	Jack posts his first win, at Osbaldeston
1993 Oct	Jack's first Novice win, at Parkgate
1994	Returns to The Royal (Dick) Veterinary Centre for more tests. Bought by Richard Holdsworth
1994 June	Jack placed in his first CCI*, at Burgie
1994 Sept	Jack's first Intermediate win, at Witton Castle
1995 May	Jack placed in his first CCI**, at Windsor
1996 June	Jack placed in his first CCI***, at Bramham
1998 May	Jack completes his first Badminton in 16th place
1998 Oct	Jack & Jeanette are awarded their Union Jack flag for the World Equestrian Games, Pratoni
1999 May	Jack places 9th at Badminton
1999 Sept	European Team Gold, Luhmuhlen
2000 Sept	Olympic Team Gold, Sydney
2001 Oct	European Team Gold, Pau
2002 Sept	World Individual Silver and Team Bronze, Jerez de la Frontera
2003 May	Jack places 3rd at Badminton, the only horse to complete on his dressage score
2003 Sept	European Team Gold, Punchestown
2004 April	Jack places 7th at Badminton
2004 Aug	Olympic Team Silver, Athens
2005 May	Jack places 5th at Badminton
2005 Sept	European Team Gold, Blenheim
2006 May	Jack places 4th at Badminton
2006 Sept	Jack places 7th at his first and only Burghley
2007 May	Jack places 14th at Badminton, after which he retires from Three Day Events
2008	After a season contesting World Cup classes Jack retires from eventing at the age of 20

"With four European Team Gold medals, two Olympic Team Silvers, one World Team Bronze, not forgetting his individual World Silver medal, Jack has entered the record books as the most medalled event horse in history."

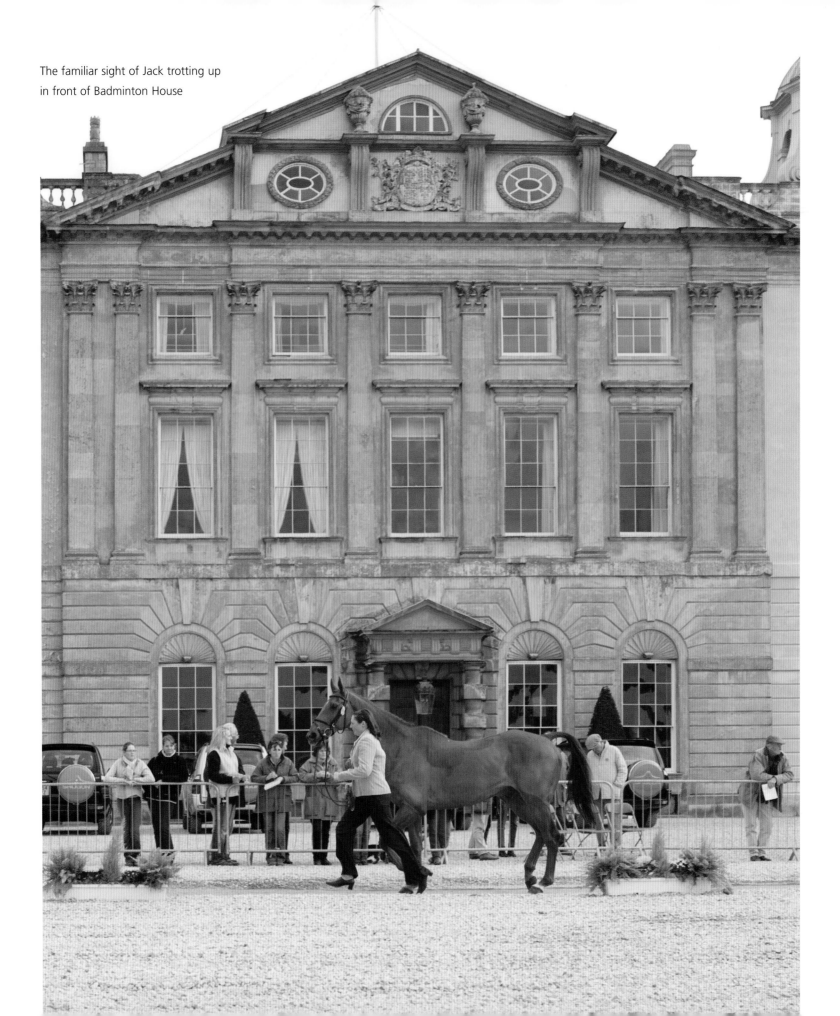

The familiar sight of Jack trotting up
in front of Badminton House